Did

BASIN

A MISCELLANY

CW00420453

Compiled by Julia Skinner

THE FRANCIS FRITH COLLECTION

www.francisfrith.com

First published in the United Kingdom in 2011 by The Francis Frith Collection®

This edition published exclusively for Bradwell Books in 2014
For trade enquiries see: www.bradwellbooks.com or tel: 0800 834 920
ISBN 978-1-84589-576-1

Text and Design copyright The Francis Frith Collection®
Photographs copyright The Francis Frith Collection® except where indicated.

British Library Cataloguing in Publication Data

Did You Know? Basingstoke - A Miscellany
Compiled by Julia Skinner
2011 photographs taken by Julian Hight

The Francis Frith Collection
6 Oakley Business Park,
Wylye Road, Dinton,
Wiltshire SP3 5EU
Tel: +44 (0) 1722 716 376
Email: info@francisfrith.co.uk
www.francisfrith.com

Printed and bound in Malaysia
Contains material sourced from responsibly managed forests

Front Cover: **BASINGSTOKE, CHURCH STREET 1904** 52129p
Frontispiece: **BASINGSTOKE, WINCHESTER STREET FROM WINTON SQUARE c1955**
B31018

The colour-tinting is for illustrative purposes only, and is not intended to be historically accurate

CONTENTS

INTRODUCTION

Until the early 1960s, Basingstoke was a small market town with a character that had gradually evolved over the years, much as any other English town. Basingstoke's main trading centre was originally centred around its market place on the higher ground above the Loddon valley, the area now known as Top of Town, but after the arrival of the Basingstoke Canal in the 1790s, and then the railway in 1839, the lower part of the town also became a business area. By the 20th century, the principal thoroughfares of the town were London Street and Winchester Street, and the two roads running north and downhill from the town centre – Church Street and Wote Street. Other roads, namely New Street, Potters Lane, Brook Street and Station Hill, also had their share of shops and other businesses.

All that was to change in the 1960s, after Basingstoke was designated a London overspill town. New housing and industrial estates were developed around the old town and thousands of people came to live and work in the area. At the same time, much of the old town was systematically demolished and rebuilt under the town development plan, giving the new-look Basingstoke a modern shopping centre, multi-storey car park and an orbital road system to take it into the modern age.

It is true that years of history were lost in the mass demolition of the old town in the 1960s and 70s, but Basingstoke gained a newer and more modern centre in the process, a process which is still continuing today, as the town continues to grow and develop into a thriving commercial and industrial centre. In recent years some of the less successful architecture of the 1960s and 70s has been demolished and more pleasing developments have taken their place. The town has been embellished with stunning pieces of modern art in a wide variety of forms, and the historic heart of the town at the Top of Town has been beautifully conserved.

BASINGSTOKE, WOTE STREET (LOWER) 1904 52130

BASINGSTOKE MISCELLANY

Around AD700, a Saxon tribe settled in the area beside the head of the River Loddon. These Saxons called themselves the 'Basingas' – the people of Basa – which is the origin of the names of both Basingstoke and the nearby village of Basing, east of the town. The Saxon name for Basing was 'Basinges', and this village appears to predate Basingstoke itself – the 'stoke' part of Basingstoke's name indicates that it was an outlying western settlement of Basa's people at Basing. Basingstoke was recorded as 'Basingestoches' in the Domesday Book on 1086, which noted that the town was already holding a market, one of only a few settlements in Hampshire to do so at that date. In 1214 the town's market day was fixed by a royal charter of King John to take place on a Wednesday, which it still remains, although a market also takes place on Saturdays now. In 1622 Basingstoke was incorporated as a borough by a Charter of James I, officially allowing it a weekly market and a twice-yearly fair. In 1641, in the reign of Charles I, Basingstoke was given a further charter which gave the town a Mayor, Aldermen and Burgesses.

BASINGSTOKE, MARKET PLACE c1955 B31008

BASINGSTOKE, CHURCH COTTAGE 2011 B31708

The making of cloth and manufacture of woollen goods appears to have been an important factor in Basingstoke's economy from the Middle Ages until the 17th century. One of the oldest surviving buildings in the town is the timber-framed Church Cottage, situated near St Michael's Church in Church Square, the earliest part of which dates from the 1520s. Church Cottage was owned in medieval times by families connected with Basingstoke's cloth industry and may have been used as premises for the dyeing of cloth, as water was channelled from the River Loddon in the past to flow beneath the building.

Another surviving historic building in the modern town is the row of eight white-painted cottages known as Deane's Almshouses at the eastern end of London Street, on the corner with New Road. They are named after their founder, Sir James Deane, who gave the money for them to be built in 1608 as homes 'for 8 poore impotent old men'. The almshouses, now listed buildings, are managed by a group of Trustees and still fulfil their original function as housing for older people.

To the north of the railway station, off Chapel Hill, is what is now called South View Cemetery. This area is believed to have been an Anglo-Saxon burial ground, and was known in earlier times as the Liten, or corpse-ground, from the old word 'lich' for a corpse. Between 1208 and 1213 the Pope put England under an Interdict, after falling out with King John over the appointment of a new Archbishop of Canterbury. During this time all churches were closed and no funerals could take place in consecrated ground, so the Liten was used as an alternative burial ground for Basingstoke's dead. The Liten was consecrated after King John made his peace with the Pope in 1213 and the Interdict was lifted, and it continued to be used as a cemetery for the town.

An awful event occurred in South View Cemetery in 1674, when Mrs Alice Blunden was buried alive there. She had partaken rather too freely of 'poppy water' (an opium-based painkiller) for a headache, and had fallen into a coma so deep that it was thought she had died. Soon after her burial in the cemetery, some boys playing nearby reported that they had heard tapping and groaning noises coming from her grave. Their story was not taken seriously at first and it was some time before her grave was opened to investigate. By then it was too late, and although it was clear that Mrs Blunden had indeed been buried alive, by this time she was definitely dead. The town was fined the then huge sum of £200 for its negligence in allowing the dreadful event to happen.

John Arlott, the famous writer, broadcaster and cricket commentator who was called 'the voice of summer', was born in the entrance lodge to South View Cemetery on Chapel Hill in 1914 – his father was the cemetery keeper and he spent part of his childhood living there. John Arlott wrote about his early life in Basingstoke in his autobiography published in 1990, which was titled 'Basingstoke Boy'.

One of Basingstoke's historic sites is the ruined Chapel of the Holy Ghost in South View Cemetery. Actually there used to be two chapels there, but little remains of the earliest structure, which dated from the 13th century and was used by the Guild of the Holy Ghost. Its surviving fragments are to the left of the tower in photograph B31724, below. The octagonal tower and ruins to the right of this view are the chapel of the Holy Trinity that was added in the 1520s by Lord William Sandys of The Vyne at Sherborne St John. By then the earlier chapel was being used as a school, so Lord Sandys built this chapel as a burial place for himself and members of his family. The chapel complex was damaged by Parliamentary troops during the Civil War, who also stripped the lead from its roof to make musket balls. Its deterioration into ruin was hastened by vandals, one of whom was Gilbert White (1720-1793), the clergyman famous for his book 'The Natural History of Selborne'; he was educated in Basingstoke, and later wrote that in his schooldays he assisted other boys in the 'wanton destruction of a part of the Holy Ghost Chapel'.

BASINGSTOKE, HOLY GHOST CHAPEL RUINS 2011 B31724

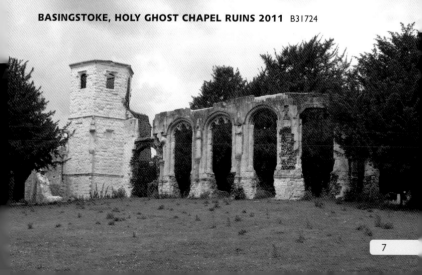

Basingstoke's parish church of St Michael in Church Square, off the lower end of Church Street, is perhaps the finest of Hampshire's Perpendicular churches. A Norman pillar close to the vestry door is a survival from an earlier church, but the oldest part of the present Grade I listed church building is the chancel, dating from 1464. The building of the nave and aisles was begun about 50 years later by Bishop Richard Fox of Winchester. Bishop Fox's shield can be seen on a corbel supporting a roof timber of the nave, commemorating his contribution to the church. The blue shield features an image of a pelican feeding her chicks with blood pecked from her breast, known as 'A Pelican in her Piety', which was used in religious art in the past as an allegorical depiction of Jesus in his sacrificial love. More recent work includes the Memorial Chapel, which was completed in 1921 in memory of the local men who died in the First World War. The church was given a Victorian restoration between 1865 and 1878, when the exterior was crowned with the 'stately diadem of pinnacled turrets' seen in photograph 42053, below.

**BASINGSTOKE
ST MICHAEL'S PARISH CHURCH
SOUTH SIDE 1898** 42053

In the mid 19th century, many historic fixtures and fittings were removed from English churches to make their interiors less 'medieval' in appearance. It was at this time that St Michael's Church in Basingstoke lost its magnificent wooden Jacobean pulpit and 15th-century font, which were removed and given to St Mary's Church at the village of Basing, where they remain. St Michael's also no longer holds The Flemish Triptych, three paintings on folding panels dating from 1549 that are believed to be the work of the Flemish artist Jan Sanders van Hemessen, a pupil of Leonardo da Vinci. This valuable piece of religious artwork was given to the church by Canon James Millward, who was rector there between 1864 and 1891, and used to be on display above the high altar, but it is now kept in Winchester Cathedral. However, the church still retains its wonderful painted Royal Arms of Elizabeth I, James I, William III, and Elizabeth II. There is also a fine piece of contemporary religious sculpture inside the church, 'Christus Rex', by Peter Eugene Ball.

A memorial plaque on the wall opposite the west door of St Michael's Church commemorates Sir James Lancaster, who was born in Basingstoke c1555 and grew up there. He became a seaman and explorer and was a founder of the East India Company, commanding the company's first voyage in 1601 which established the trade route between Britain and the East Indies. As one of the chief directors of the East India Company, most of the voyages of the early 17th century to India and in search of the Northwest Passage (a sea route around North America through the Canadian Arctic connecting the North Atlantic to the Pacific Oceans) were undertaken under his sponsorship and direction, and in 1616 a channel north-west of Baffin Bay in the Canadian Arctic was named Lancaster Sound by William Baffin in his honour. Closer to home, Lancaster Road in South View in Basingstoke was also named after him. Sir James Lancaster died in 1618, and left provision in his will for the establishment of a charitable trust for the benefit of poor people in Basingstoke.

Another charitable bequest to the town was made in 1646, when Richard Aldworth left money for the foundation of a Blue Coat School in Cross Street. Aldworth was a wealthy London merchant who had also been a governor of Christ's Hospital School in London. After his death he left money for the foundation of two similar schools in Reading, which had been his birthplace, and Basingstoke, which had been the birthplace of his mother, Jane South, whose family was prominent in the local wool trade. The boys had to wear similar attire to those of Christ's Hospital – a long blue coat, yellow stockings and buckled shoes. The Blue Coat School in Basingstoke originally educated ten boys from 7-16, teaching them how to write, read the Bible and do simple arithmetic. Each year one of the boys would leave the school, having been apprenticed to a tradesman in the town. The school was incorporated into the National Schools system in the 19th century and was rebuilt, but it closed in 1879 and the school building was later demolished. Its site in Cross Street is now marked by a small statue of a Blue Coat Boy commissioned by Basingstoke Heritage Society in 1994; it was cast from a mould of the statue of a Blue Coat Boy at the Blue Coat School in Reading, which still exists today.

The name of Richard Aldworth and his contribution to the educational heritage of Basingstoke is commemorated in the name of Aldworth Science College, formerly Richard Aldworth Community School, in Western Way in South Ham, a secondary school with Specialist Science College Status. When the school was opened in 1963, a stone plaque from the old Blue Coat School building was incorporated into the main entrance. Richard Aldworth is also commemorated in the name of Aldworth Crescent in South Ham.

**BASINGSTOKE, CROSS STREET, THE BLUE COAT BOY STATUE
2011** B31704

One of the most bitter conflicts of the Civil War of the 17th century took place just east of Basingstoke, at Basing House in Basing, the home of John Paulet, 5th Marquess of Winchester, who was staunchly loyal to Charles I and the Royalist cause. Surrounded by strong walls, Basing House became a stronghold of Royalist support in the area, and Paulet and his forces defended the house for the king during a siege by Parliamentary forces that lasted nearly three years. It appears that soldiers from the two sides met in battle in Basingstoke at some time, as depressions caused by musket balls can be seen on the outer walls of St Michael's Church, especially the south wall. Eventually Oliver Cromwell arrived with around 8,000 men of his New Model Army. Cromwell attacked the house with artillery, then on 14th October 1645 his forces stormed the house and breached its defensive walls, overwhelming the 300-strong Royalist garrison and killing many civilians as well as soldiers. The Marquess of Winchester was found hiding in a bread oven and taken to the Bell Inn in Basingstoke (the HSBC Bank now stands on the site in London Street) where he was kept prisoner in the cellar before being sent to London for trial. Also taken prisoner was the architect Inigo Jones, who had taken refuge in the house; a news sheet of the time reported that he had lost all his clothes, and was carried away from the house naked and wrapped in a blanket.

Cromwell then allowed his troops to ransack and plunder the house. Shortly afterwards the house caught fire and burnt down, probably because a smouldering fireball from the assault was left unattended. Tragically, the Royalist soldiers who had not been killed in the assault were being held prisoner in the cellars of the house when the fire began; unable to escape, they perished in the blaze. After the fire, Cromwell ordered the remains of the building to be razed to the ground. The site of Basing House is now a ruin and only the cellars and foundations of the Tudor mansion remain.

After being captured in the assault on Basing House, John Paulet, Marquess of Winchester was sent to London for trial. However, the charges against him were later dropped, and he was released. After John Paulet's death, his son Charles became the new Marquess of Winchester. In the 1680s he built a new Paulet family mansion on the Hackwood estate, a few miles south of Basingstoke, which the family also owned. In the early 19th century a later member of the family, the first Lord Bolton, enlarged and extended the residence, resulting in the mansion at Hackwood Park that stands today.

Perhaps it was a member of the Paulet family who commissioned one of the great treasures in Basingstoke's Willis Museum at the Top of Town, the Basing House 'Raised Work' Embroidery, which is believed to date from the 1660s. It is a wonderful example of English 'raised work', also known as 'stump work', in which a three-dimensional 'raised' picture is achieved by stitching the design over areas padded with wool or cotton. The motto of the Paulet family at the time of the Civil War was 'Aymez Loyaulte' (love loyalty), and this is featured on the wall surrounding the grand house at the top left of the embroidery, which is assumed to represent Basing House, whilst the man shown to the left of the canopy may represent John Paulet, 5th Marquess of Winchester, who defended the house for the Royalist cause during the Civil War. Charles I was executed by order of Parliament in 1649 and the king who is depicted in the embroidery sitting under the canopy is thought to represent his son Charles II – his return from exile in France and restoration to the throne in 1660 is symbolised by the image of the sun coming out from under the clouds.

Whilst he was directing the siege and assault of Basing House in 1645, Oliver Cromwell stayed in Basingstoke at the Falcon Inn in London Street – the site is now marked by a plaque on what is now 13 London Street near the NatWest Bank. From there on 14th October 1645 he sent a letter to the Speaker of the House of Commons, addressed from Basingstoke, informing Parliament that Basing House had been taken.

London Street that leads into the Market Place at the Top of Town used to be one of the main roads into the town centre. The photograph below shows how it looked around 1930; it was pedestrianised in 1976. The striking building with a large Tuscan portico on the right of the photograph dates from 1800. It was originally the Congregational Church, but is now the United Reformed Church. Sited in front of the church nowadays is one of the striking pieces of modern artwork that adorn modern Basingstoke. The bronze statue by Mike Smith is an abstract work symbolising how a family unit can be strengthened by drawing on the traditional values of the church.

**BASINGSTOKE, LONDON STREET
c1930** B31301

Up to fifty stagecoaches would travel along London Street most days in the 18th and early 19th centuries, and Basingstoke's inns prospered on the coaching trade until it was killed off by the coming of the railway in the mid 19th century. One of the town's busiest coaching inns was the Red Lion Hotel, still in business in London Street. Others have now gone, such as the Angel Inn in the Market Place at what is now Top of Town. In the 1920s the Barclays Bank building was constructed on its site. Behind the Angel were some Assembly Rooms, and tradition says the novelist Jane Austen (1775-1817) attended dances there; Jane spent the first 25 years of her life at Steventon, west of Basingstoke, where her father was the rector, and she was a frequent visitor to the town. However, it is now thought more likely that she attended the Basingstoke Balls held in Assembly Rooms above the old town hall that stood in the Market Place to the east of where Lloyds TSB Bank is now; that town hall was demolished in 1832, to be replaced by the building that now houses the Willis Museum. Other former coaching inns that still stand but have changed their names were the Feathers at the top of Wote Street, now known as Laarsen's (seen on the right of photograph B31737 on page 17) and the Wheatsheaf in Winton Square, now known as the Winton.

Winton Square, the junction of Winchester Road, Sarum Hill and Winchester Street, is named after Winton House, a handsome Georgian house that stands opposite the Winton pub. Originally a wealthy merchant's house, it later became a girls' boarding school kept by Ann and Susan Dusantoy who were friends with Jane Austen, so she may have been a regular visitor there. The house gained the name that also became the name of the square at the opening ceremony of the school. One of the people who attended was the Bishop of Winchester, who suggested that the building was named after the Latin abbreviation for 'Winchester' used after his Christian name as part of his official signature.

BASINGSTOKE, WOTE STREET
THE CORN EXCHANGE AND
THE TOWN HALL 1898   42052

In 1724, Daniel Defoe recorded in his 'Tour Through the Whole Island of Great Britain' that Basingstoke 'has a good market for corn'. This trade continued to grow, and in the 1860s an impressive Corn Exchange was built at the top of Wote Street. Prior to this, the local factors bought and sold corn from stalls on the lower ground floor of the Town Hall. After the Corn Exchange ceased trading in grain, the building was used for various purposes, including a roller skating rink from 1910-13, and in 1913 it became the Grand Exchange Cinema, the first cinema in the town. The building suffered a major fire in 1925 but was rebuilt, and in 1951 it became the Haymarket Theatre. It still continues in that role, seen on the left of photograph B31737, below. In its early days the Corn Exchange was also the home of the town's horse-drawn fire engine, which was kept in its basement. This role ended in 1913 when the fire brigade moved into a purpose-built fire station in Brook Street, complete with Basingstoke's first motorised fire engine.

BASINGSTOKE, WOTE STREET
2011 B31737

BASINGSTOKE, WOTE STREET c1900 5336

Photograph 5336 (above) of upper Wote Street was taken around 1900, looking up towards the Market Place, with the Corn Exchange (now the Haymarket Theatre) on the right, and now-lost clock tower of the old Town Hall (now the Willis Museum) looming on the skyline. On the left of this view is the Emmanuel Church of Lady Huntingdon's Connexion (a nonconformist religious sect), and its manse on the left. The church originally dated from 1775 but was rebuilt in 1802 and then enlarged and restored in 1874. The church and its manse were demolished in the 1960s and the site was redeveloped into shop premises. The site of the church is now commemorated with a modern sculpture, The Church Stone by Michael Pegler, seen in the modern photograph B31739 on the opposite page which was taken from the opposite direction, looking north down Wote Street towards the entrance into Festival Place. Hand carved out of silver grey granite, The Church Stone stands almost 3 metres high and features an image of a mother and child on one side.

Basingstoke grew over the centuries from a settlement in the Loddon valley to a town that expanded to cover the hills on both sides of the river. When the Market Place was established on the higher ground on the southern side of the valley, centred around the town hall, or 'mote hall' ('mote' meant 'meeting'), it became the centre of the town and trade grew around that area, now known as the Top of Town. In past times this area of Basingstoke was known as the 'Upland', and the area at the bottom of the town, around lower Wote Street etc, was known as the 'Soke'. In the 19th century 'Upland' and 'Soke' were names used by local people as a way of differentiating between 'them' and 'us'.

There are several theories about the origin of the name of Wote Street. One is that it was originally 'Mote Street', a reference to the 'mote hall' that it led to in the Market Place. Another theory is that it may originally have been called Oat, or Ote, Street, but as 'oats' are pronounced 'woats' in the Hampshire dialect, this local pronunciation eventually became the official name of the street.

BASINGSTOKE, WOTE STREET, THE CHURCH STONE 2011 B31739

The building in the Market Place at the Top of Town that houses the Willis Museum used to be Basingstoke's Town Hall, built in the 1830s to replace the 17th-century Town Hall that stood to the east of Lloyds TSB Bank. It was originally open on the ground floor to provide space for market traders, but in 1865 the ground floor was enclosed. The building officially ceased to be the Town Hall in 1981, after new Civic Offices were built in New Road, and became the Willis Museum in 1984, named after George Willis (1878-1970) who did much to preserve and record the history of Basingstoke and was the founder of the town's first museum, in New Street, in 1931. He had a keen interest in local botany, history and archaeology, and many of the items he collected in his lifetime are on display in the museum. George Willis had a watch and clock repair and jewellery business at number 3 Wote Street, next to what is now the Laarsen's pub – a replica of the shop as it appeared in his lifetime has been erected at the Milestones Museum at the Leisure Park off Churchill Way West.

BASINGSTOKE, THE MARKET PLACE AND THE TOWN HALL c1955 B31026

The photographs of the former Town Hall in the Market Place in this book show it with the impressive four-faced clock tower that was added to the building in 1887, to commemorate Queen Victoria's Golden Jubilee. It replaced a smaller structure built with the Town Hall in 1832 and was the gift of the then-mayor, Lt. Col John May (1837–1920), popularly known in the town as 'The Colonel'. A wealthy member of the family that ran the town's biggest brewery, John May became mayor of Basingstoke six times between 1883 and 1902. He was a very benevolent mayor, financing a number of public works, including paying for the construction of a wing of the cottage hospital; he also donated the bells of All Saints' Church in Southern Road and the bandstand that now stands in the War Memorial Park (see page 23) as well as funding the erection of the clock tower on the Town Hall. Sadly, the clock tower had to be taken down in the 1960s when it was found to be unsafe, although a part of the clock remains in the second-floor window over the entrance porch of the building.

Another of Colonel May's gifts to the town was the May's Bounty Cricket Ground on Bounty Road. Bounty Road was originally part of Southern Road, but the section running alongside the cricket ground was renamed after Colonel May bought the land and donated it to the town, in memory of his 'bounty' (generosity). The Bounty Inn on the corner of Bounty Road and Council Road used to be called The Cattle Market Inn because it appears that a cattle market was held in the area in the past, but was renamed in the 1950s to commemorate John May's gift of the cricket ground land. For many years the pub's signs featured a ship, presumably because the brewery that owned it thought the name of the pub related to the famous mutiny on the 'Bounty' ship, but in recent years they have been replaced with new signs featuring portraits of Colonel May, to celebrate the pub's connection with Basingstoke's great Victorian benefactor.

BASINGSTOKE, HACKWOOD ROAD 1904   52127

Throughout the 18th century, roads were improved by turnpike trusts set up by investors who paid for a stretch of road to be put into good repair, and then charged a toll from traffic using it. There were various toll gates in Basingstoke, and one was in Hackwood Road. The old toll house was the white cottage on the left of photograph 52127, above. Both cottages in this view were demolished in the 1920s, and the building seen in photograph B31723 on the opposite page, bottom, now stands on the site of the old toll house, to the right of the Hackwood Road entrance into the War Memorial Park.

The bandstand in the War Memorial Park (seen on the left of photograph B31723, opposite) was originally erected in the Fairfields Recreation Ground, south of Fairfields School, in the late 19th century. It was a gift to the town from Lt. Col John May, and is seen in photograph 42033 on the opposite page, top, in its original position and condition. When the War Memorial Park was laid out in the 1920s in memory of the local people who died in the First World War, the bandstand was moved there.

BASINGSTOKE
FAIRFIELDS RECREATION GROUND
THE BANDSTAND 1898 42066

BASINGSTOKE, HACKWOOD ROAD
THE ENTRANCE TO WAR MEMORIAL PARK 2011 B31723

BASINGSTOKE, THE BOARD SCHOOL, COUNCIL ROAD 1898 42063

Photograph 42063 (above) shows the Board School at Council Road in the Top of Town, better known now as Fairfields School, which opened as the town's elementary school in 1888. The school comprised two buildings, that on the left was for juniors, and that on the right was for seniors. The senior building was also used as a boarding school for a time, for both male and female pupils. The school was built on land that was used as the site of a sheep fair in the past, known as Fair Close, which gave the school its name. Board Schools were run by a board of elected members. They could charge fees, but the schools were also partly funded by Government grants; however, this grant funding was dependant on regular attendance by the pupils, and the children at Fairfields School were presented with attendance medals as an inducement to keep them coming to school.

Amongst those educated at Fairfields School in the past were George Willis, Basingstoke's local historian and the founder of the town's museum, John Arlott, the writer, broadcaster and popular cricket commentator famous for his rich Hampshire accent, and – less impressively – Ruth Ellis (née Nielsen), who in 1955 became the last woman in Britain to be executed by hanging, for the murder of her lover. Although she was born in Wales in 1926, Ruth Ellis's family later moved to Basingstoke and she attended Fairfields Senior Girls' School until she was fourteen. She moved with her family to London the following year, in 1941.

As a result of falling school rolls, the two departments of Fairfields School amalgamated in the 1980s into Fairfields Primary School, based in the larger of the two buildings, the former senior school, which is the building to the right of photograph 42063. The former junior school, the building to the left of the photograph, is now Fairfields Arts Centre, housing Basingstoke's art gallery.

As well as the Haymarket Theatre and Fairfields Arts Centre, Basingstoke also has another wonderful cultural venue in The Anvil on Churchill Way. The Anvil was completed in 1994 and was so-named because its unusual shape (especially when viewed from the western approach) looks like the horn end of a blacksmith's anvil; its name also recalls the town's industrial and agricultural heritage. The auditorium seats 1,400 and was specifically designed to be the ideal shape and size for a first-class concert hall. The Anvil is famous for its near-perfect acoustics, and was reviewed in The Times newspaper as 'a regional venue well worth the journey', with acoustics 'as warm as an Italian courtyard'. When The Anvil was built, a number of site-specific artworks were incorporated into the design, including a light sculpture in the foyer by Martin Richman, which slowly changes colour, and external neon sculptures by Peter Freeman.

Basingstoke joined the Canal Age in 1794 with the opening of the Basingstoke Canal, linking Basingstoke with London via its junction with the River Wey navigation at West Byfleet. It was built with the intention of bringing coal from London and taking grain and timber back, boosting local trade by providing cheap transport for agricultural goods and locally produced timber, bricks and chalk. The last commercial craft on the canal operated in 1950, and the canal became derelict. The Surrey and Hampshire Canal Society was formed in 1966, and restoration work began after Surrey and Hampshire County Councils purchased the canal in 1974. The canal was reopened in 1991, and is again navigable from the Greywell Tunnel, five miles east of Basingstoke, to the River Wey. The last section of the canal into Basingstoke from Greywell has now been lost, but two miles of its route can be followed along the Basingstoke Canal Heritage Footpath from near Festival Place to the grounds of Basing House at Old Basing.

BASINGSTOKE, 'SAILING BY STARS' 2011 B31728

BASINGSTOKE, WOTE STREET c1955 B31020

Basingstoke's canal heritage was the inspiration for Sarah Tombs' sculpture 'Sailing by Stars', which stands near the railway station in Alencon Way.

Wote Street once led down from what is now the Top of Town to the Basingstoke Canal basin, which was roughly where the cinema in Festival Place is located now. After the canal closed, the canal basin became White's Timber Yard and later still it became the site of the bus station. Photograph B31020 (above) shows a view taken in the 1950s from lower Wote Street looking towards Station Hill. The town's two leading cinemas used to be located here, the Waldorf and Savoy. The Waldorf Cinema, seen on the right of this view, was later called the Cannon. The small building seen in the centre of this view was public toilets, and the hornbeam tree behind it was known as the Reformers' Tree because it was a gathering place for political meetings in the past. This whole area was demolished to make way for the new town centre development of the 1960s, and the Reformers' Tree was cut down in 1967.

Basingstoke had important leather, malting and brewing industries in the past, but during the 19th century the Basingstoke Canal and the coming of the railway helped increase trade and triggered the development of other industries in the town, leading to its gradual expansion. The London and South Western Railway arrived in 1839 from London, and within a year Basingstoke was connected by rail to Winchester and Southampton. In 1848 a rival company built a branch from Reading, and in 1854 a further line was built to connect the town to Salisbury.

By 1860, within twenty years of the railway's arrival, the town's manufacturing growth and increased employment opportunities meant that more houses had to be built, suitable for the increased amount of workers coming to Basingstoke to work in local businesses. The small houses were built between the railway line and Worting Road, in an area that was later called 'Newtown' and is now known as Brookvale. It was probably this area that Thomas Hardy was describing when he wrote about Basingstoke in his novel 'Jude the Obscure' of 1895, in which the town was disguised as 'Stoke-Barehills': 'There is in Upper Wessex an old town of nine or ten thousand souls; the town may be called Stoke-Barehills. It stands with its gaunt, unattractive ancient church, and its new red brick suburb…The most familiar object in Stoke-Barehills nowadays is its cemetery, standing among some picturesque medieval ruins beside the railway…'.

The 'Brook' in the names of Brook Street, Lower Brook Street in the Brookvale part of the town refers to the River Loddon, and what is now the site of the Victory roundabout on Churchill Way used to be an area called 'Noah's Island', so named because it was surrounded by branches of the river.

In the 19th century Basingstoke began to move into industrial manufacture with a number of successful companies based in the town, such as Wallis & Steevens, the agricultural engineers, who had a large works at the bottom of Station Hill. Wallis & Steevens began as Wallis & Haslam, producing agricultural equipment including threshing machines in the 1850s. They went on to produce stationary steam engines in the 1860s, traction engines in the 1870s, and then, in the 1890s, the steam road rollers for which they were famous. They moved into the production of diesel and petrol vehicles in the 20th century. Wallis & Steevens moved to a site at Daneshill in the 1960s, but ceased trading in 1981.

Another famous name in Basingstoke's history started in 1898, when John Isaac Thorneycroft & Co moved to Basingstoke from Chiswick and began production of steam-powered lorries. Thorneycroft's grew to become the town's largest employer, and by the 1960s the works site on Worting Road covered 63 acres. They also made cars between 1903 and 1912, but gave this up to concentrate on building their successful commercial and military vehicles. By the mid 20th century they were particularly well known for the Mighty Antar, a heavy-duty lorry used by the British Army for several decades as the standard tank transporter, Queen Mary low loaders and bren gun carriers. The Basingstoke works also designed and made the prototypes for the 'Terrapin' Mk 1, an amphibious transport vehicle that was a significant part of the success of the D-Day Normandy landings of the Second World War, although they were actually produced by Morris Motors at Oxford. Thorneycroft's merged with AEC Ltd of Southall in the 1960s, then the firm was taken over by the Leyland group in 1968. In 1973 Eaton's acquired the factory, closing it in 1991. The Thorneycroft's factory that was once so important to Basingstoke was demolished in 1995, and replaced by a supermarket.

Both Wallis & Steevens and Thorneycroft's had a reputation for reliable products and sound engineering, and are names that have a proud place in Basingstoke's history. A number of vehicles made by both companies are preserved in the Milestones Museum at the Leisure Park off Churchill Way West.

BASINGSTOKE, WINCHESTER STREET c1955 B31017

The world-famous Burberry clothing company was founded in Basingstoke in 1856 when 21-year-old Thomas Burberry opened an outfitting business in Winchester Street. Mr Burberry had noticed that shepherds' smocks became waterproof as a result of absorbing oil from the wool of their sheep. Working on this idea, he devised a method of waterproofing yarn before weaving it to produce a waterproof cloth that was more pleasant to wear than rubberised fabric. He set up a factory in the town to manufacture his waterproofed cloth, which he called 'gabardine', an old medieval word which originally meant a long, loose cloak or gown, but later came to be used for a rain cloak or protective smock. The overcoats made with this fabric shed rainwater instead of absorbing it, and were lightweight and comfortable but still warm to wear in winter. They proved so popular that they became known as 'Burberrys'. In 1905 Thomas Burberry's shop premises in Winchester Street burnt down, and an impressive new premises was built on the site. The former Burberry emporium still stands in Winchester Street – it is the building with the long frontage and two striped 'towers' on the left of photograph B31017 (above).

Burberry cloth was manufactured in several workshops around the town in the company's early years, but in 1892 Thomas Burberry built a large factory in London Street. Photograph 52128 (below) shows what used to be part of Hackwood Road in 1904 – all the buildings in this view were demolished in the 1970s for the construction of the New Road link with Victoria Street and the new Civic Offices. In the middle of the row of buildings on the left hand side is an arched doorway with the initials B.Y.P. picked out in lighter coloured bricks. This was the entrance for workers going into the Burberry factory behind these houses, where raincoats and overcoats were made from 1892 until 1957, after which Burberry's manufacture was transferred to London; the initials stood for Burberry's Yarn Proof.

Another Basingstoke company making outdoor wear in the past was founded by John Mares, who had been an apprentice at Burberry's. The John Mares clothing factory in New Street was particularly famous for its raincoats, known as 'Peltinvains'. The company closed down in the 1950s.

BASINGSTOKE, HACKWOOD ROAD 1904 52128

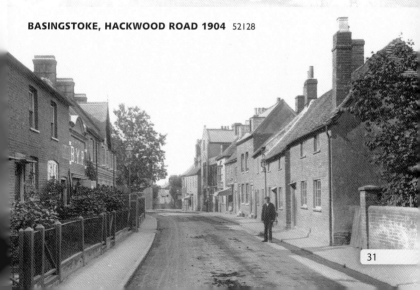

BASINGSTOKE, WINCHESTER STREET c1960 B31048

Another company that started in Basingstoke in the 19th century and went on to become a household name was the Milwards chain of shoe shops. Alfred Milward is said to have made his first pair of shoes in the building known as The Warren in Church Street, at the corner with Cross Street. He had a hawker's licence and started his business in 1857 by travelling around the area with a handcart, selling his boots and shoes door to door. As the business expanded, he bought in stocks from wholesale footwear houses around the country. He opened his first shop in Winchester Street in Basingstoke and the second one in Reading, and by 1957, one hundred years after Alfred Milward started his business, there were Milwards shoe shops in 39 towns in the south of England. The Milwards company was taken over by Clarks Shoes in the 1990s.

As shown in this atmospheric view of upper Church Street in 1904, many of the main streets of 'old' Basingstoke were quite narrow, and would have been unsuitable for modern traffic even if the town had not undergone its major redevelopment scheme in the 1960s and 70s. Upper Church Street was pedestrianised in 1988. Behind the children is a shop awning with the sign 'Griffin – Pork Butcher' at number 17 Church Street; as Griffin Brothers, the business closed down in 1968 after trading from there for 72 years. Their speciality was cooked meat, pies, and the 'Basingstoke Pork Sausage'. The next building down from Griffin's was what was then called the Black Boy Hotel in Church Street; it later became the Hop Leaf public house, then McCarthy's Bar and is now (2011) the Censo bar. The Black Boy Hotel's emblem used to be a statue of a small Negro boy standing beside a tobacco coil, advertising that tobacco was sold there; the statue can now be seen in the Willis museum.

BASINGSTOKE, CHURCH STREET 1904 52129

BASINGSTOKE, THE VIEW DOWN CHURCH STREET c1960 B31036

By the 1930s a number of companies had moved to the town, such as the leather goods manufacturer Percy Fisher in Kingsclere Road, the aeronautical instrument firm of Kelvin, Bottomley and Baird in Winchester Road and the pharmaceutical firm of Eli Lilly, which in 1939 moved into its six-storey building high on the hill overlooking the town, off Kingsclere Road. The Eli Lilly factory is the large white building in the top left corner of photograph B31036 (above), showing the view over the town just before the redevelopment of the town centre began in the 1960s. The Eli Lilly factory was built in Art Deco style in 1939, just before the Second World War began. The gleaming white exterior of the factory would have made it an easy target for enemy bombers during the war, so it was covered with camouflage paint for the duration of hostilities. Eli Lilly and Co is still in Basingstoke, but is now based in Lilly House in Priestley Road (formerly Norfolk House, the AA headquarters from the mid 1990s until 2003), although the old Art Deco premises off Kingsclere Road still stands.

During the Second World War, Thorneycroft's contributed a great deal to the war effort, producing around 13,000 vehicles and various types of equipment for the three Armed Forces, including guns, gun carriers, mobile cranes and water carriers. Also doing its bit for the war effort was the firm of Kelvin, Bottomley and Baird (later Smith's Industries) in Winchester Road, which supplied aeroplane instruments and other equipment for the RAF and Royal Navy, including altimeters, compasses, and barometers.

Basingstoke's industries made it a potential target for enemy action in the Second World War, and there were several air raids on the town. One of the worst raids took place on 15th August 1940, when a number of houses in Church Square near St Michael's Church were badly damaged by German bombs, and eleven people lost their lives; one of the casualties was a young lady who was killed by a bomb as she was running out of her father's shop to give aid to the injured. It seems that the Germans were trying to hit the railway goods yard but missed their target, dropping the bombs in the heart of the town and also in Burgess Road, where four more people were killed. A few weeks later another attack saw a bomb dropped on St Vincent's, a private school in Cliddesden Road; two ladies were tragically killed, but luckily the school children were out playing in the War Memorial Park at the time of the attack, or otherwise the casualties would have been far worse. In the mid 1950s an area of Church Square was laid out as a garden of remembrance for those who died in the 1940 bombings.

In 1944 the comedy film 'He Snoops to Conquer' starring George Formby was filmed in Basingstoke, which was used as the location for the fictional town of 'Tangleton'. Set in the aftermath of the war, the plot concerned corrupt town council members who were doing nothing about the lack of housing and other facilities in the war-damaged town, and how they were foiled by George Formby's character, the Town Hall odd-job man. Church Square featured in several scenes in the film, where the bomb damage was still much in evidence.

Basingstoke was developing fast even before it was designated
as a London 'overspill' town in the 1960s. Its population doubled
between 1951 and 1961 as people flocked to the area for its good
employment prospects, and by 1960 Basingstoke had several new
housing estates, such as South Ham, Oakridge, Harrow Way, and
the Berg. The shopping area of the 'old' town, mainly based around
Winchester Street, London Street, New Street, Church Street and
Wote Street, was a busy place, but the increasing amount of motor
traffic in the town's narrow streets was a problem, and there were few
places to park. Before the town centre was redeveloped, and before
Basingstoke had any sort of bypass or ring road, traffic came through
the town on the two main streets that joined the Market Place,
London Street and Winchester Street. Photograph B31011 (below)
shows a white-gauntleted policeman directing traffic on point duty
in the Market Place in the 1950s. There was always a policeman on
point duty there on market days, Wednesday or Saturday, when the
town centre became particularly busy and congested with traffic.
They worked four-hour shifts, between 6am and 10pm.

BASINGSTOKE, MARKET PLACE c1955 B31011

Basingstoke changed for ever in the 1960s, after a tripartite agreement was made between London City Council, Hampshire County Council and Basingstoke Borough Council to accommodate some of London's 'overspill' population. A number of farms around the town were compulsorily purchased, and new housing and industrial estates were built to accommodate the influx of thousands of people from London who came here to live and work; the names of some of those farms were retained in the names of the estates, such as Buckskin and West Ham. This plan to expand Basingstoke meant that a drastic transformation of its town centre and road systems had to take place. The Borough Council initiated a major development programme to make Basingstoke a modernised town that could cope with the needs of its greatly increased population, and a long period of mass demolition and rebuilding began. Much of the old town between Church Street and Wote Street was flattened to make way for a modern shopping centre and multi-storey car park, and other parts of the town were cleared for new road systems.

Part of the redevelopment scheme for the town included a network of ring roads and roundabouts. Modern Basingstoke now has so many roundabouts that it has been nicknamed 'Doughnut City'. Some of them have been given names that reflect the town's history, such as the Victory roundabout on Churchill Way, which is named after the Victory pub that used to stand here (which was in turn named after Lord Nelson's flagship at the battle of Trafalgar in 1805), and the Venture Roundabout at the bottom of Hackwood Road, which recalls the name of the Venture bus company, Basingstoke's main bus company from 1926 until it was taken over by the Wilts & Dorset bus company in 1950.

BASINGSTOKE, ALL SAINTS' CHURCH 2011 B31703

One of the saddest losses suffered by the town during its redevelopment was the demolition in 1967 of the beautiful Church Street Methodist Church, which stood opposite St Michael's Church. Built in 1905, its design was reminiscent of the Holy Trinity Church in Sloane Street in London. The church went to make way for the New Shopping Centre, and all that remains is a plaque marking its site in the pavement near the Church Street entrance to Festival Place. However, the town does still have another architectural gem of a church in All Saints' Church at the corner of Southern Road and Victoria Street, described by Malcolm Parker in his book 'Basingstoke' in the Images of England series (2007) as 'the most architecturally important of Basingstoke's churches'. All Saints Church was designed in Gothic Revival/Arts & Crafts style in 1915 by Temple Moor (1856-1920). It is widely regarded as one of the best 20th-century churches in the country. There is also much to admire inside the church, including the bronze 'Head of Christ' by the renowned artist Dame Elisabeth Frink on the west wall and three stained glass windows, designed by Cecil Collins and produced by Patrick Reyntiens.

For a long time, the new look modern Basingstoke that emerged from the building rubble of the 1960s and 1970s was the butt of jokes – unkindly referred to as only fit for accountants to live in. This was continuing a trend of making fun of the town that had begun many years earlier – for instance, in Gilbert and Sullivan's comic opera 'Ruddigore' of 1887, the character Sir Despard Murgatroyd agrees with his wife Margaret to use the word 'Basingstoke' as a code word for something boring and calming to bring her back to her senses whenever she is danger of relapsing into madness. The finale of 'Ruddigore' also ends with the lines:

> *'We shall toddle off tomorrow,*
> *From this scene of sin and sorrow,*
> *For to settle in the town of Basingstoke.'*

However, this propensity to make fun of Basingstoke is unfair to the town of the 21st century. The Basingstoke of today has excellent cultural and sporting facilities, and some of the worst examples of 1960s architecture have been redeveloped in recent years – for example, the central part of the 1960s' shopping centre was rebuilt and extended in 2002, opening as the much more attractive Festival Place (see page 42).

Central Basingstoke has two further shopping centres, The Malls and the Top of Town. The Top of Town is the historic heart of 'old' Basingstoke, and is now an attractively pedestrianised area with many interesting old buildings, particularly in Church Street, Winchester Street and London Street – look up above the modern shop and business frontages at street level and you will see the remains of Basingstoke's older era, delightfully described as looking 'rather like old ladies who have found to their horror that they have come out without their skirts' by Anne Hawker in her book 'The Story of Basingstoke' (1984). The Malls area has recently undergone a major refurbishment and redevelopment and been given a clear glass canopy roof, making it a bright and stylish part of town with a new gateway entrance from Alencon Link and the railway station.

Close to the new entrance to The Malls is one of the striking modern artworks that adorn modern Basingstoke, 'L'Arc' by David A Annand (see opposite). The work consists of two male figures cast from bronze and stainless steel that stand on either side of the road at Station Link, near the junction with the road up to the station. Each figure is holding a curved pole; the two poles would form an arch over the road if they were extended and joined together, symbolising Basingstoke's close relationship with its European twin towns.

The design of the 'L'Arc' artwork has a similarity to the famous 'Hands of Victory' war memorial in Baghdad in Iraq, of two hands grasping sword blades that form an arch over the road, which has a link with Basingstoke. The sword blades for the monument were cast in Iraq, but the two giant hands grasping the blades were actually made in Basingstoke in 1988, cast in bronze at the world-famous Morris Singer Foundry that was based at Wade Road from 1967 to 1999.

The Morris Singer Foundry at Basingstoke also cast The Triumphal Gates that stand at the New Road end of London Street near the Deane's Almshouses. Designed by Peter Parkinson and forged by blacksmith Richard Quinnell, the striking piece of sculpture forms an impressive entrance to the pedestrianised part of Top of Town. It also features 16 delightful decorative panels depicting stories and events in Basingstoke's history, such as the burial of the unfortunate Mrs Blunden (see page 6) and the Balloons Over Basingstoke hot-air balloon festival that took place in Basingstoke each summer for many years.

BASINGSTOKE, ALENCON LINK STATUE 'L'ARC' 2011 B31702

Festival Place is a vibrant shopping and leisure centre of the town that opened in 2002. The River Loddon runs beneath its site before emerging into Eastrop Park, and was the inspiration for a number of pieces of artwork that were specially commissioned to enhance its external areas, including neon light effects, water features and imaginative seating. A theme incorporated into the artwork is a flower that used to be so common in the Loddon Valley that it was named the 'Loddon Lily' ('Leucojum Aestivum'); it is also known as the Summer Snowflake although it actually flowers from April to May. Although it is now becoming rare elsewhere in the country, the Loddon Lily still grows in profusion in the Basing Fen, a natural wetland area around the River Loddon in Old Basing which can be reached by following the Basingstoke Canal Heritage Footpath from Eastrop Park.

BASINGSTOKE, FESTIVAL PLACE 2011
B31742

BASINGSTOKE
LOOKING NORTH WEST FROM EASTROP WAY 2011 B31725

A short walk from Festival Place is Eastrop Park, which was laid out for the town during the 1960s redevelopment. Here the River Loddon re-emerges after flowing underground beneath the town centre. The western end of the park is accessed from Festival Place by the Eastrop Link underpass, embellished with a series of decorative steel panels inscribed with lines of poetry inspired by the river. A plaque on the wall of the underpass commemorates the Basingstoke Canal which came into the town in this area (Festival Place covers the land occupied by the canal wharf and basin), accompanied by representations of the canal tokens used to pay the navvies building the canal in the 1790s, when official coinage was in short supply. The Basingstoke Canal tokens were worth one shilling, and could be used as currency in local pubs.

The River Loddon runs through Eastrop Park before flowing away to eventually join the Thames. How fitting that Eastrop Park is such a popular place for local people to come and enjoy themselves, beside the river that caused Basa's people to settle here so many centuries ago and found the town we now call Basingstoke.

SPORTING BASINGSTOKE

The May's Bounty Cricket Ground in Bounty Road is the home ground of the Basingstoke and North Hampshire Cricket Club. The earliest recorded cricket match played there by a Basingstoke team was in 1817. The ground was formerly known as The Folly, but became known as May's Bounty after Lt. Col John May bought the land for the town for use as a cricket ground in the 1870s. The special atmosphere and setting of the May's Bounty ground has always made it a popular venue for both players and spectators. May's Bounty Cricket Ground has hosted county cricket matches since 1906, only intermittently until 1966, but then annually until 2000. In 2001 Hampshire moved all county games to the Rose Bowl at Southampton, but in 2008 one county fixture a year was moved back to Basingstoke to be played at May's Bounty. Nearly all the great Hampshire CC's cricketers of the 20th century played at the ground, including Robin Smith (born 1963), who recorded the county's highest individual score there, 179, against Nottinghamshire in 1996.

Basingstoke Town Football Club was founded in 1896. The club's nicknames are 'The Stokes' and 'The Dragons' the latter being a reference to the club badge which features St Michael standing over a dragon, which is the symbol on the coat of arms of the Borough of Basingstoke and Deane. The club's motto is 'Vestigia Nulla Retrorsum', which means 'No stepping back'. Basingstoke Town currently (2011) play in the Conference South. To date, the club has won the Hampshire Senior Cup four times, the most recent being the 2007-08 season. The club's biggest ever win was in the FA Cup 1st Qualifying Round in 1976, beating Chichester City 10-0. The club's record goalscorer to date is Paul Coombs, who scored 164 times for the club between 1991-99.

Basingstoke Rugby Football Club (Rugby Union) was formed in March 1948. It has had several homes over the years, but moved to Down Grange in 1971. The club runs four senior sides, an Academy and youth rugby, a women's XV and a girls' team. The club was awarded the RFU Seal of Approval in 2007. To date (2011) the club has won the Hampshire Cup twelve times, most recently in the 2009-10 season.

HAUNTED BASINGSTOKE

Many theatres around the country are said to have resident ghosts, and Basingstoke's Haymarket Theatre is no exception. According to the website of the Hampshire Ghost Club (www.hampshireghostclub. net), the restless shades that roam the building include a little girl, a man wearing a black cape and tricorn hat, and a Grey Lady with her hair dressed in old-fashioned style in a bun, who wears a long grey gown with a bunch of keys hanging from her waist.

The historic Red Lion Hotel in London Street, a former coaching inn, is said to be haunted by the ghost of a woman affectionately known by the staff as 'Molly'. Another pub in the town reputed to be haunted is the White Hart on London Road, which is said to be haunted by a couple of ghosts, one male and one female. Staff have reported seeing strange ghostly figures walking around at night, and over the years several landlords of the pub have been woken at night by the unexplained sound of beer barrels being rolled around outside the building, although no one was there. Other people have reported hearing the sound of disembodied footsteps following them around the building…

BASINGSTOKE, LONDON ROAD AND THE WHITE HART INN 1898
42067

QUIZ QUESTIONS

Answers on page 50.

1. In which of William Shakespeare's plays is Basingstoke mentioned?

2. What is the link between Basingstoke and the classic children's books 'The Borrowers' by Mary Norton, and 'Worzel Gummidge' by Barbara Euphan Todd?

3. What sports are played, respectively, by the Basingstoke Bisons, the Basingstoke Bluefins, and the Basingstoke Zombie Horde?

4. With which 3 European cities is Basingstoke twinned?

5. Whereabouts in Basingstoke can you find what is probably the oldest wedding cake in the world?

6. Whereabouts in the town can you find a doorway surrounded with fruit?

7. What is the link between Basingstoke and the song 'Do-Re-Mi' in the film and musical 'The Sound of Music'?

8. Photograph B31733 on the opposite page shows one of Basingstoke's landmark buildings, The Tower at Skyline Plaza, formerly Alencon House, which was used as offices by IBM. It has now been converted into residential apartments and had an extra three storeys added to the original structure. It is now the tallest building in Basingstoke, just topping Fanum House, the AA headquarters office building, which used to hold that record. Why might you need to look out for the Tower building if you were an aeroplane pilot?

9. Who raced a Ford Fiesta car through the interior of Basingstoke's Festival Place in November 2008?

10. Who – or what – is 'Poppy', and whereabouts in Basingstoke can you find her?

BASINGSTOKE THE TOWER AT SKYLINE PLAZA 2011 B31733

RECIPE

HAMPSHIRE PICNIC CAKE

The mixture of spices and honey gives this cake a lovely flavour.

> 115g/4oz butter or margarine, softened to room temperature
> 225g/8oz caster sugar or soft brown sugar
> 3 eggs, beaten
> 175g/6oz self-raising flour
> ¼ teaspoonful salt
> ½ teaspoonful ground nutmeg
> ½ teaspoonful ground cinnamon
> 2 tablespoonfuls milk
> 2 tablespoonfuls runny honey
> ¼ teaspoonful bicarbonate of soda
> 175g/6oz raisins or sultanas
> 175g/6oz chopped walnuts
> 6-8 walnut halves, to decorate

Pre-heat the oven to 160°C/325°F/Gas Mark 3 (slightly less for a fan oven). Grease and line a 900g (2 lb) loaf tin.

Sift the flour, salt and spices together into a bowl. In a separate bowl, cream together the butter or margarine and sugar until light and fluffy. Beat in a little of the beaten eggs and then some of the flour mixture. Repeat alternately until all is used up. Warm the milk very slightly in a pan, add the honey, then sprinkle in the bicarbonate of soda, stir until dissolved and add to the cake mixture. Add the chopped walnuts and dried fruit, and combine it all together well. Turn the mixture into the cake tin and bake just below the centre of the pre-heated oven for 1-1¼ hours, then lightly press the walnut halves into the top of the cake and bake for a further 40-45 minutes. Cover the top of the cake with kitchen foil if it seems to be browning too quickly. Leave the cake to cool in the tin before turning out on a wire rack and leaving to cool completely.

RECIPE

HAMPSHIRE DROPS

115g/4oz butter or margarine,
  softened to room temperature
115g/4oz caster sugar
1 egg, beaten
115g/4oz plain flour
115g/4oz cornflour
1 level teaspoonful baking powder
A little jam or butter icing (optional)

Pre-heat the oven to 190°C/375°F/Gas Mark 5 and grease a baking sheet.

Sift together the flour, cornflour and baking powder. In a separate bowl, cream together the butter or margarine and sugar until light and fluffy. Beat in the egg, a little at a time. Add the flour mixture, and mix together well to form a soft dough.

Flour your hands. Take rounded teaspoonfuls of the dough and roll them in your hands to form small balls, about the size of a golf ball (this amount should make 12-15 Hampshire Drops). Place the balls on the baking tray, spaced well apart, and bake in the pre-heated oven for 10-12 minutes, until they are risen and firm to the touch, but not over-browned. Leave to cool and firm up on the baking tray for a few minutes, then cool on a wire tray.

These can be eaten as they are, as small biscuits, or sandwiched together with a little jam, or perhaps some butter icing made by beating icing sugar into softened butter, in a proportion of one part of butter to two parts of icing sugar, plus a little milk, and a few drops of vanilla extract if liked.

QUIZ ANSWERS

1. Basingstoke features in Shakespeare's 'King Henry IV' (Part II), in act 2, scene 1:

   Lord Chief-Justice: 'Where lay the king last night?'
   Gower: 'At Basingstoke, my lord.'

2. The Basingstoke artist Diana Stanley, who died in 1975, was a famous illustrator of children's books, including Mary Norton's 'The Borrowers' and Barbara Euphan Todd's 'Worzel Gummidge'. She also wrote a wonderful book about the town as it was before its redevelopment in the 1960s, illustrated with her own paintings, called 'Within Living Memory', published in 1967. Some of her paintings of the town are on permanent display in the 'Story of Basingstoke' gallery in the Willis Museum.

3. The Basingstoke Bisons play ice hockey; the Basingstoke Bluefins are the town's swimming team; and the Basingstoke Zombie Horde play American Flag Football.

4. The Borough of Basingstoke and Deane is twinned with three European towns: Alencon in France, Braine-L'Alleud in Belgium and Euskirchen in Germany. Their names are recalled in several road names, ie Alencon Way, Braine-L'Alleud Road and Euskirchen Way.

5. The shopping precinct of Potters Walk is on the site of Potters Lane which used to run between Church Street and Wote Street. In 1898 Charles Philpott opened a confectionary and baker's shop in Potter's Lane and placed a wedding cake in a sealed round glass case in the shop window as an example of his skills. The cake remained in the window after his two daughters took over the shop, and stayed there until the shop closed in 1964 and the Potters Lane buildings were demolished as part of the town

redevelopment. The cake eventually found its way to the Willis Museum, where it can be seen on display. Now over 110 years old, it has been the subject of several conservation programmes, and its icing is not exactly sparkling white any more, but the intricate icing detail and decoration remains a testament to Mr Philpott's art.

6. The doorway to Lesser Market on Wote Street, next to the Haymarket Theatre, is surrounded by a decorative stucco frieze of moulded and coloured fruit. Lesser Market was erected in the 1860s to link the newly built Corn Exchange with the Town Hall, where the ground floor (where market traders formerly did business) had recently been enclosed. The frontage of Lesser Market is now a Grade II listed building.

7. The song 'Do-Re-Mi' puts music's tonic sol-fa system into song form, teaching the notes of the major musical scale to the children in the story. The tonic sol-fa method was developed to teach children to sing and read music by John Curwen, who was the Minister of what is now the United Reformed Church in London Street in Basingstoke from 1838 to 1841. A plaque on the church commemorates the link.

8. The Tower at Skyline Plaza in the heart of Basingstoke is the tallest building on the flight path from Heathrow Airport in London and New York.

9. Jeremy Clarkson, of BBC 2's 'Top Gear' television show. An episode of Top Gear was filmed in Basingstoke in November 2008 in which Jeremy Clarkson 'tested' the new Ford Fiesta by racing around Festival Place in the early hours of the morning, whilst being chased by a Chevrolet Corvette.

10. 'Poppy' is the name of the sculpted figure of a ballet dancer that stands outside the Anvil Theatre. It was the work of Tom Merrifield, and was erected there in 1996.

HAMPSHIRE DIALECT
WORDS AND PHRASES

'Feeling lear' - feeling hungry.

'Cackleberries' - eggs.

'Sherricking' - a good telling off.

'Puggled' - confused or daft, as when someone does something silly.

'Not too dusty' - when something is okay, acceptable.

'Winty' - weather that is a bit windy and a bit wintery.

'Foisty' - damp or musty.

'Ampshire Og' - Hampshire Hog, a Hampshire-born local.

'Ackled' - not working properly, as in 'It doesn't ackle'.

'Gallibagger' - scarecrow.

'Shrammed' - cold, shivery, frozen through.

BASINGSTOKE, MEN TALKING IN COUNCIL ROAD 1898 42063x

FRANCIS FRITH

PIONEER VICTORIAN PHOTOGRAPHER

Francis Frith, founder of the world-famous photographic archive, was a complex and multi-talented man. A devout Quaker and a highly successful Victorian businessman, he was philosophical by nature and pioneering in outlook. By 1855 he had already established a wholesale grocery business in Liverpool, and sold it for the astonishing sum of £200,000, which is the equivalent today of over £15,000,000. Now in his thirties, and captivated by the new science of photography, Frith set out on a series of pioneering journeys up the Nile and to the Near East.

INTRIGUE AND EXPLORATION

He was the first photographer to venture beyond the sixth cataract of the Nile. Africa was still the mysterious 'Dark Continent', and Stanley and Livingstone's historic meeting was a decade into the future. The conditions for picture taking confound belief. He laboured for hours in his wicker dark-room in the sweltering heat of the desert, while the volatile chemicals fizzed dangerously in their trays. Back in London he exhibited his photographs and was 'rapturously cheered' by members of the Royal Society. His reputation as a photographer was made overnight.

VENTURE OF A LIFE-TIME

By the 1870s the railways had threaded their way across the country, and Bank Holidays and half-day Saturdays had been made obligatory by Act of Parliament. All of a sudden the working man and his family were able to enjoy days out, take holidays, and see a little more of the world.

With typical business acumen, Francis Frith foresaw that these new tourists would enjoy having souvenirs to commemorate their days out. For the next thirty years he travelled the country by train and by pony and trap, producing fine photographs of seaside resorts and beauty spots that were keenly bought by millions of Victorians. These prints were painstakingly pasted into family albums and pored over during the dark nights of winter, rekindling precious memories of summer excursions. Frith's studio was soon supplying retail shops all over the country, and by 1890 F Frith & Co had become the greatest specialist photographic publishing company in the world, with over 2,000 sales outlets, and pioneered the picture postcard.

FRANCIS FRITH'S LEGACY

Francis Frith had died in 1898 at his villa in Cannes, his great project still growing. By 1970 the archive he created contained over a third of a million pictures showing 7,000 British towns and villages.

Frith's legacy to us today is of immense significance and value, for the magnificent archive of evocative photographs he created provides a unique record of change in the cities, towns and villages throughout Britain over a century and more. Frith and his fellow studio photographers revisited locations many times down the years to update their views, compiling for us an enthralling and colourful pageant of British life and character.

We are fortunate that Frith was dedicated to recording the minutiae of everyday life. For it is this sheer wealth of visual data, the painstaking chronicle of changes in dress, transport, street layouts, buildings, housing and landscape that captivates us so much today, offering us a powerful link with the past and with the lives of our ancestors.

Computers have now made it possible for Frith's many thousands of images to be accessed almost instantly. The archive offers every one of us an opportunity to examine the places where we and our families have lived and worked down the years. Its images, depicting our shared past, are now bringing pleasure and enlightenment to millions around the world a century and more after his death.

For further information visit: www.francisfrith.com

INTERIOR DECORATION

Frith's photographs can be seen framed and as giant wall murals in thousands of pubs, restaurants, hotels, banks, retail stores and other public buildings throughout Britain. These provide interesting and attractive décor, generating strong local interest and acting as a powerful reminder of gentler days in our increasingly busy and frenetic world.

FRITH PRODUCTS

All Frith photographs are available as prints and posters in a variety of different sizes and styles. In the UK we also offer a range of other gift and stationery products illustrated with Frith photographs, although many of these are not available for delivery outside the UK – see our web site for more information on the products available for delivery in your country.

THE INTERNET

Over 100,000 photographs of Britain can be viewed and purchased on the Frith web site. The web site also includes memories and reminiscences contributed by our customers, who have personal knowledge of localities and of the people and properties depicted in Frith photographs. If you wish to learn more about a specific town or village you may find these reminiscences fascinating to browse. Why not add your own comments if you think they would be of interest to others? See **www.francisfrith.com**

PLEASE HELP US BRING FRITH'S PHOTOGRAPHS TO LIFE

Our authors do their best to recount the history of the places they write about. They give insights into how particular towns and villages developed, they describe the architecture of streets and buildings, and they discuss the lives of famous people who lived there. But however knowledgeable our authors are, the story they tell is necessarily incomplete.

Frith's photographs are so much more than plain historical documents. They are living proofs of the flow of human life down the generations. They show real people at real moments in history; and each of those people is the son or daughter of someone, the brother or sister, aunt or uncle, grandfather or grandmother of someone else. All of them lived, worked and played in the streets depicted in Frith's photographs.

We would be grateful if you would give us your insights into the places shown in our photographs: the streets and buildings, the shops, businesses and industries. Post your memories of life in those streets on the Frith website: what it was like growing up there, who ran the local shop and what shopping was like years ago; if your workplace is shown tell us about your working day and what the building is used for now. Read other visitors' memories and reconnect with your shared local history and heritage. With your help more and more Frith photographs can be brought to life, and vital memories preserved for posterity, and for the benefit of historians in the future.

Wherever possible, we will try to include some of your comments in future editions of our books. Moreover, if you spot errors in dates, titles or other facts, please let us know, because our archive records are not always completely accurate—they rely on 140 years of human endeavour and hand-compiled records. You can email us using the contact form on the website.

Thank you!

For further information, trade, or author enquiries
please contact us at the address below:

**The Francis Frith Collection, Oakley Business Park,
Wylye Road, Dinton, Wiltshire SP3 5EU.**
Tel: +44 (0)1722 716 376 Fax: +44 (0)1722 716 881
e-mail: sales@francisfrith.co.uk **www.francisfrith.com**